quiet orient riot

nathalie khankan

quiet orient riot

OMNIDAWN PUBLISHING
OAKLAND, CALIFORNIA
2020

Cover art by: Bashir Makhoul, *One drop of my tears*, 2000
Photograph, 200 cm x 200 cm

Cover and interior set in Poiret One, Kabel LT Std, and Electra LT Std

Cover and interior design by Gillian Olivia Blythe Hamel

Library of Congress Cataloging-in-Publication Data

Names: Khankan, Nathalie, 1972- author.
Title: Quiet orient riot / Nathalie Khankan.
Description: Oakland, California : Omnidawn Publishing, 2020. | Summary:
  "quiet orient riot is a book about birth regimes and the politics of
  reproduction. Tracing the immaculate conception of a child through to
  her birth, it unspools the many ways that liturgical commands and an
  intense demographic anxiety affect a journey towards motherhood. What
  does it mean to bear a Palestinian child in the occupied Palestinian
  territory, enabled through contingent access to Israel's sophisticated
  fertility treatment infrastructure? How do you bear a body whose very
  creation is enabled by the pronatalist state, yet not recognized by it?
  How do you end up a national vessel? Are we all national vessels? While
  the journey is specific and localized, the larger questions that emerge
  from these poems are not: what kind of language may hold precarious
  life? What kind of poem may see a body held inside a body through
  emergency, diminishment and into resistance, bloom? Importantly, and
  over and above demographic and religious imperatives, these poems are
  concerned with other kinds of worship, bowing to a "chirpy printed
  sound," "what grows in the rubble," and "the capacity for happiness
  despite visual evidence." Where you look, there are water holes for the
  thirsty and a grove of "little justices.""-- Provided by publisher.

Identifiers: LCCN 2020023020 | ISBN 9781632430830 (trade paperback)
Subjects: LCGFT: Poetry.
Classification: LCC PR9142.9.K47 Q54 2020 | DDC 821/.92--dc23
LC record available at https://lccn.loc.gov/2020023020

Published by Omnidawn Publishing, Oakland, California
www.omnidawn.com   (510) 237-5472
10 9 8 7 6 5 4 3 2 1
ISBN: 978-1-63243-083-0

An arresting debut collection, Nathalie Khankan's *quiet orient riot* is like no other book of poems. Truly original in its approach to the poem and to saying anything, *quiet orient riot* stages a revolution against the spiritual and actual reduction of a people. She calls this resistance "demographic intifada." Though revolution is never pretty, Khankan makes it impossible for us to look away. One poem begins, "the way it sounds it's maissoun coming for dinner | she always says that we should stop holding our breath for justice | she says enjoy the little justices instead." The search for "little justices" configures one narrative anchor across the book, and when they emerge—these little justices—they do so desperate and breathless as if all existence relies on them. This is because violence and loss permeate the landscape. We understand this from Khankan's images of grief. They speak to the failure of utterance amid chaos: "this is a picture of three men standing up coiling father | his hands empty & empty." It's altering to read a world where even the size of justice must be shrunken.

Almost immediately, the poems create a disorientation in their seduction. In this, we are the temporarily blindfolded lover who experiences syntax disorders that limp around inside of us alongside the quotidian utterances that accompany everyday violence: "someone loved is dying." The poems perform the kinds of language disjuncture compelled by unending war; rationalities that defend disposability of humans; and, one's own pregnant vulnerability. "What'll happen," she writes, "if we return to the needle type sentence"? Yet, the tension between desired language and possible language is one of the primary ways Khankan illustrates how persistent state violence invades the interior spaces of people. Brilliantly, she manages to write about conflict by creating innovative language structures and architectures for the poem that reflect the claustrophobic textures of invasion itself.

The gentle radiance and radiation of *quiet orient riot* are likewise perfect conflicting modalities for this meditation on the possibility of birth within a landscape where "the human count is a crucible." The poems steadfastly resist metaphor as if to say, nothing can stand in for the thing itself, or as if to say the thing itself stripped of artifice needs no new dressing. Khankan's is a poetics of powerful imagistic nakedness. Here is where craft and urgency come together to create a voice that is both uncanny and iridescent. Here is where we're compelled to come together, not in chorus, but in guttural gesture. If we need any book of poems now, it's *quiet orient riot.*

Dawn Lundy Martin
Author of *Good Stock, Strange Blood*
Judge of the Omnidawn 1st/2nd Poetry Book Prize

All poetry is about the body, and the body is never one, always a multitude held together by variable processes, biologic and terrestrial. In *quiet orient riot*, Nathalie Khankan speaks through "all macrocosms of the uterine" beyond the frozen embryos in state of the art fertility centers. Pregnant in Palestine, she found herself "where birth counts," where birth is a regime: the state of Israel serves a woman's will to conceive in the same breath it dominates Palestinian existence, administers to Palestinians conditional access to life: "in this expired area/ i'll bear another child," the mother says. The book is inevitably packed with oracular and biblical echoes. No body seems possible without them in the Israel/Palestine chimera. But Khankan maintains a clarity of broken language in the shadows of the extant, doesn't sacrifice tenderness, insists on deep listening to "hear [a baby's] eyelashes grow." *quiet orient riot* asks subversive questions about the body, more daring than what we find in the news: "[How] to be a mother and not also a national vessel"? When is common decency an alibi to the ethics of settler colonialism? When is liberalism a state of the art? Khankan's poem liberates itself from the state that approved it as a demographic, a solidarity annexed. It's impossible to escape this book's power and its aporia and unsolved tensions. A flowering wound, it's a Palestinian book in Empire. And yes, it does sing.

Fady Joudah, author of Footnotes in the Order of Disappearance

Poetically and politically, *quiet orient riot* is a powerful book. In it Nathalie Khankan inhabits the unbearable contradictions between living in Ramallah under the Occupation in a period that saw the 2008 bloody assault on Gaza, and being able to conceive through an Israeli hospital's fertility treatments. Drawing ironic analogies between "body growth" and "body count," Khankan moves between the lyrical expression of a personal struggle to have a child and the dry citation of death and birth demographics in Israel and Palestine, leaving the gaping contrasts between them unresolved. Throughout, she lists instances of what she calls "little justice," tokens of agency and resistance, and the joys of everyday life. And rather poignantly, she links quotations from the Qur'an with texts from the Hebrew Bible and Midrash about Hannah's barrenness and Maryam's labor pangs, holding out women's linguistic and embodied courage as a reminder of the joint cultural heritage of Palestinians and Jews.

Chana Kronfeld, author of The Full Severity of Compassion:
The Poetry of Yehuda Amichai *quiet orient riot* explores what it means to have a child in the occupied Palestinian territories, a Palestinian child, a child that was possible because of the Israeli state's investment in assisted reproductive technology. It is a poem about holding tight to the intimacy and love for this child, a love that is independent of claims made by an occupying military and state. These are quiet poems, reminders of how to hold tight to deep loves in difficult times. And so they are at the same time, necessary poems, ones attentive to experimentalism's narrative possibilities. It's a book that will stay with you long after you have read it.

Juliana Spahr, author of *That Winter the Wolf Came*

The danger of delivery made courageous with this *quiet orient riot* where her "nerve endings are maternal." In Palestine a woman tries to correspond with Darwish and is driven to the far reaches of form. Khankan gives birth to a geopolitics of intimacy and exile that has no known beginnings or future. This is the work that changes you, that demands that you too, give, unyieldingly, as you are.

Sarah Riggs, author of *Pomme & Granite*

for basil

& for yara

& for luma

to say i once wrote an email to mahmoud darwish i don't know if he saw about being newly arrived in the occupied territories | before i knew to call it territory | THE BREAD IS FLAT IN MY HAND & it's a flawless kilometer to a friend's house | a taxidermied giraffe in qalqilya i haven't seen yet & a progressive progesterone protocol i haven't tried yet & he's not yet a dead poet

to say i'm in a position on the brown sofa on the fifth floor in *bayt al-shami*
& cold | i go between hussein's blue light & wringing towels of tepid
water | anticipate one land | in that position on the sofa & that national
question | when i'm done writing chapter four the poet's dead | he's dead
in houston during a poet's heart's operation | basil is away when news
from texas | salim says everyone will be at al-manara square | it's a literary
history | it's a poet's funeral | it's a QUIET ORIENT RIOT

said on these storied soils | don't spoil any seed | there is no pure race | a
bride is still bridal | a checkpoint is STILL TORN HILL | in just a few weeks
topographical categories shift & our bodies move toward a lid with a
tighter seal | with the hill gone another concrete tower erupts & the
militarized sanitized | it's a border crossing running through continuous
land | if i get married i will get stuck here & my wedding *thōb* against
the bodies of busses jamming here | if i bear a child my engorged breasts
here | the human count is a crucible

i leave the brown sofa | on the white ford transit simple heat | before we get off the bus to cross the qalandia checkpoint the song is *yā musāfir waḥdak* | human beings are plenty | hostile the turnstiles | soon i'll break into a fact on the ground | A DINOSAUR IN THE FIELD & a hebrew university | light touches a chin first | it's a professor & he looks at me surprised like that | he once worked on medieval arabic travel graffiti with a dane so i'm easy to like | dedications from names of writers i know multifarious & connected | the dinosaur speaks | *is your habibi palestinian* | it took a long time to get here | *many people have died on this side* | & i didn't get here | *promise me you're only here to write* the way it sounds it's maissoun coming for dinner | she always says that we should stop holding our breath for justice | she says enjoy the little justices instead | those teeth of hers are monumental | i've always wanted an ambrosial smile & subtle glottal stops | from here you may proceed straight & only look back once | on the corner by lambada video next to *kull shi shahi* A YOUNG ARAFAT GLINTS IN THE AFTERNOON SUN | in it it feels like home & handsome patriotism | this is area [a] & the margins are utterly regrettable the palestinian central bureau of statistics presents the following information about palestinians at the end of twenty fourteen

the projected number of palestinians in the world is twelve point ten million of whom four point six two million are in state of palestine one point four six million in israel five point three four million in arab countries and around six hundred seventy five thousand in foreign countries

the total fertility rate declined during twenty eleven to twenty thirteen to four point one births compared with six point o births in nineteen ninety seven in gaza strip the rate was four point five births compared to three point seven births in the west bank during twenty eleven to twenty thirteen

palestinians in the world

we live in a city on a hill & it belongs to god & shuttered cinemas | soils

shimmer toward something grand | shattering in many parts | & cumin

is pervasive | this is ramallah you see & much shapes up & many are

digging | WE CONSUME SUMMER & habitable evenings | my ovaries

have been in the hands of men on both sides | my sister skypes between

children from the left land | my follicles are not yet purring | she says *of*

course nothing will happen to me

where are the cartographers | when qalandia was a byzantine bath a holy

city was close | when qalandia was an international airport for prominent

guests A CITY WAS CLOSE & OPEN | a future mother-in-law with short

hair wore a fitted dress as she waved to & never returned from | *wallahi*

she looked just like jackie k

in your imagination this tract of land is big with eyes glassy | this land fits
neatly into other pockets of land | one time into belgium | two times &
more into togo | this land is coming home | messy & the way HUMAN
RIGHTS WORK | belt of orange & flower dusty thursday | siblings moving
into childhood homes in tulkaram & bir nabala | this land is things
coming apart & some reunions | this land is the understanding in which
we work | it's a consensus it folds | neatly into other lands

the world in palestinians

in the palestinians world

a little justice: THIS CHIRPY PRINTED SOUND when i leave the library

with kifah | every day a tiny goodness aggregates

the electricity is back & the main functions of our local attachments |
before abu basil left british mandatory palestine he rested on a rock with
his eyes closed | the sun leaks from his cheekbones & his knitted vest
is a color we can guess | sometimes closed eyes in a picture will tell a
terrible story | the abundance we would know was known by none | the
crude birth rate was known | the crude deaths were crude | to release
THE SURFACE I'M GRIPPING i flex other muscles | in doctor shukri's
office something has already been | it's an east myriad & kindred | *i vow
to you what is in my womb*

MEANWHILE INTERVALS | we move beyond the microbiological & stratified reproduction | in this fecundity a distribution | along all lines of state & military | all macrocosms of the uterine | infrared hierarchies of semen seemingly | as figure three point two shows | the mean number of ever-born children to women | noticeably the mean of ever-born children remains fixed & in table three point four | ever-married & currently married women are distributed by number of children ever-born | mean number of palestinian children ever-born & living every year on the eve of the day of the declaration of independence of the state of israel the israeli central bureau of statistics publishes its latest demographic snapshot

in twenty sixteen there are six million three hundred seventy seven thousand jews living in israel making up seventy four point eight percent of the population and one million seven hundred seventy one thousand arabs making up twenty point eight percent of the population and three hundred seventy four who describe themselves as other

jew arab other

INSIDE AN OVULATION & a centennial population policy my mother

calls with dream | *we were in the same house* | it's a morning melting &

lidded | *why didn't i see you* | in the garden everything is devoid of demise

| much kindly made walnut | outside the garden something has already

been | all life may be deserved | land may be severed | or severe & saved

| words of hebrew i knew were so few

HEBREW I KNEW | settle | viable | *shalom* | *machsom*

kristine writes *i'm in vallarum* | each roof is a roof of thatch each sleep is a sleep unadorned | we send fiery first maps & string | ramallah __ vallarum | we are both alone & a part of something sonorous | A NAME IS DOING HARD WORK in places | what's a name supposed to do | i tell kristine what's afoot in significant territory & she repeats what we already remember of finding | colors erupt & recline against rocks & thyme | *vallarum* i say *it's closer now to the first rain* | *vallarum* i say *here comes an olive season & the end of euphemism* | & every friday in this territory another peppery breakfast by another salim

now hannah she spoke in her heart   she said   master of the universe of
all that you created in woman   you did not create anything for naught
eyes with which to see   ears with which to hear   a nose with which to
smell   a mouth with which to talk   hands with which to do work   feet
with which to walk   and breasts with which to nurse   these breasts that
you placed on my heart   what for   not to nurse from them?

vallarum i say *i wish i were a farmer's daughter* | a permanent alien farmer's daughter | & you can call me something enchanting | hold me till morning | when i wake up early i pee in one of these four tinny pails | i spread fingers across the sky & braid all day | palestinian yellow flax | MILK VETCH | apple of sodom | i don't wonder where the rent boys go after light | i don't wonder when the missing girl returns | the said is sayable it will all be mine | *nashīd ṣaghīr samak kabīr* | ṣmall anthem big fish retrieve | transfer | HEBREW | KNEW TOO | freeze the embryos

may after may we remain on the bank | we leave & come back | we leave
one of us behind | one time i will leave the territory & a bridge will close
| basil is there to pull the plug on the refrigerator but he doesn't | how do
you raid a refrigerator | i gather my belonging in an urban center | it's a
different opening | IT'S A LIVING SITUATION | remorse return rejoice
| the headlines stay & human cargo | we wish we could master longer
lines | the walnut tree keeps giving | a little justice: arabic is a beautiful
language

occupied repose | where the outer edge of this settlement | where the wall barrier | where oslo is metonym for peace | for all of us a case to be made of sentient life | MY BODY IS ON THE WAY | & peace will be on you the day you will be born | we saw bodies along the way | how does it feel to live where history is made | where demographic intifada | how does it feel to conceive where birth counts

news that break | ronit from the fertility clinic at the hadassah medical
center | endometrium at eight millimeter | LEADING FOLLICLES at
eighteen millimeter | mashallah mashallah |

ما شاء الله
ما شاء الله

thistle thirst we have | our patience is seasonal & occasional | THIS LAND IS FABULOUS PRIORITY | i'd like to cope by doing whatever feels right at the moment & not be confined | we have one looming catastrophe & the number of our unborn children | we have arabic auricles & atriums | what'll happen if we return to the needle type sentence | what if we behave rattily | go on deserve your land | a little justice: the unoccupied moon that returns shining into our bucket | of course our children everywhere

STREETS THAT NARROW on the other hand | it's a pool of hips | this is a picture of three men standing up coiling father | his hands empty & empty | there's no trace of saccharine in the teas of gaza | there is nowhere safe to hide | strident gets us through twenty one days | we see raw & wrapped truncated winds | to say i see country with some war | *although seabird populations can withstand the failure to produce young in one or even a few years without suffering severe population-level consequences the loss of adults has an immediate and long-lasting impact on population dynamics* | we meet & i see you | your head piles in my lap like a geometric slab of gorgeous rock | the quarries slimming around us | *even a small decrease in adult survival rates may cause population decline* | it's easy to wish away a winter of dying & processing disorders other arab jew

arab other jew

jew other arab

i see only the girl in khan younis cupping a small thing | i dismiss all culture outside this wound | me part wanting what words plenitude | what completes & combines concern for her | all the measures we take & hold for a while | in those eyes which overture or ritual of care suffices | she has a brother & a brother | THEY LIE SQUARE & ALTERED | doesn't one of her loved ones | i see only the girl's hand's small cupping | a function of the memory of pleasure & warm content | language is a perpetrator | define dearly sentence in khan younis today | fresh beginning young house | now my members make themselves everyone the war is over LET'S TRANSFER SOME EMBRYOS | kristine erupts again

from a roofless room in vallarum | *there is something out there i'm trying*

to catch she says | & *just now daniel is scattering cow piss on his grass*

fields | something in the old country | after twenty one days of mental

aberration we've grown alert | skies quiet | a family named samouni

collects its living | the timing is the timing | *he ploughs them right away*

so the unpleasant smell of rotten eggs won't linger

i call hadassah fertility clinic & the nurse flaunts the flag | dr o returns to jerusalem from gaza city in time to perform embryo transfer | it's a tide pool of white | eggs & phosphorous | i call basil to deliver me out of imminent complicity & maternal possibility | hammoudeh lost his toes bleeding | SHE FED HIM LIKE A BABY BIRD | dandelion & concrete strings between ramallah & vallarum don't help | someone loved is dying | it's a day & there's no rumor of its end the counting soars then stops | dim is the sun when you pick me up | to say it's a sky | we drive west to yaffa our eyes are open | it's a war & it's end & beginning of low intensity interlude | your shirt is open too | it's a hair of mine on your chest | when it's my time i insist on the following pain strategy | breathing oxygen | could all life detour like this | old city sounds like ducks falling | i miss my territory but it was never my territory | i throw my light into the pail of pooled light | you & i land & long | it's a small long land | SOMETHING YOU CROSS SHOULD BE A RIVER

to say AT THE FOOT OF STARS IT'S AN OPERATION OF DUST |
flailing & scentless | it's a kind of laughter | in a world of fewer babies
i can even begin to tell you how lucky we soon were | crested child
girl | conceived inside two population biologies with reproductive
rates | you can imagine us quantifying our fecundity | *for seabirds the
aggregation of large portions of the adult population in colonies means
that a single catastrophic event can kill a large segment of the local
breeding population* | you can imagine us contemplating factors that
will influence nest survival

TO SAY THE LATITUDES ARE CLEARLY | the possibility of an available

birth city multiplies | we will count the contractions & their pronatal

contingencies | bethlehem two checkpoints away | jerusalem one |

ramallah none | when the time comes i'd like to move around as much

as i need to | i'd like not to be confined | this near millennia of sweet

talking assisting women | i'd like to cope | a row of shared rooms &

separating curtains | it's a newborn father | his hands are handsome out

of his pockets & we pretend the mount of olives near | it's a drawn & taut

curtain | i ask hala when time comes if i can squat behind the curtain |

she says *no supine* | supinely only

and the pains of childbirth drove her to the trunk of a palm tree she said
o i wish i had died before this and was in oblivion forgotten but he called
her from below her do not grieve your lord has provided beneath you a
stream and shake toward you the trunk of the palm tree it will drop upon
you ripe fresh dates so eat and drink and be contented.

in nineteen forty three the chief rabbi of palestine yitzhak halevi herzog

wanted jewish families to be fruitful & multiply & replenish the earth

| much later you were born on lettered territory | APPLE CHEEKED IN

YOUR CHOSEN BODY | it turns out it was also herzog not nobel laureate

shmuel yosef agnon who wrote the nineteen forty eight prayer for israel |

our divine guardian rock & redeemer of | *bless the state of* | *the beginning*

of our redemption | how it matters the beginning of a redemption came

from the lips of the rabbi not the novelist

between dusk & somewhere i churn | into my awfully shapely hands she comes as eyes | on these soils something has already been | there's behind this well a shine | there's behind this shine a wall | & all the morning mourning & making of fall | I WAIT FOR NO ONE NOW | there's behind this wall grass | there's behind this grass hope o my lord i have vowed to you what is in my womb to be dedicated to your services accept this from me   verily all-hearer the all-knowing then when she delivered her she said o my lord i have delivered a female child we take the carried & the KISSED TO BE WEIGHED | three thousand six hundred forty five grams & now she is counted | we swim in a sea of radiant participles | we don't want to give her laden names | we resist an ever-quotable ending | to say we exist & die to introduce even a minimal change in the strength of the state | to say we reproduce in equal measure & not at the same time | whether the proportion of palestinians in the west bank | whether jews in judea & samaria | whether our replacement level grows | our handsome eulogy for the carried tiny throbs | count this child girl | count her on this side | this is her first birth world out of maternal technology conceived matter | to say the child girl is |

EARLY & ALREADY i bear the born | i carry the carried | uphill & downhill

& around she's a sleeveless slippery sun drenched demographic | the bus

is a vehicle & its number is eighteen & its license plate green | i run

after it & sit in it & look out the window with someone born | the lifted

is light & there's no shade on the way home from an ancient city | *i say*

about love what it brings me without you responding with exact words |

an unmistakably sleeveless newborn | i kiss the kissed & all her unruly

birthplaces | bethlehem west bank middle east | she's held & before the

rain | *that's the relief*

the way we went down the hill | the way basil was all spine & departure | the way we settled | in the crowd in my direction the very thought of it | the running the other way | fadwa's clothes lines in the courtyard | THE WAY SHE MUST'VE LEARNED TO WRITE there | the ripples in the sheets waft the sooner | the dreary dormant headlines | the gates & traumas open only inward | the names of the operations | derivative struggles & in some of the stories there's always a girl

THE CAPACITY FOR HAPPINESS DESPITE VISUAL EVIDENCE IS GREAT | you have begun to worship what grows in the rubble | i dream of multiple sweet children in diffident t-shirts | count more than twenty impossibles | ahmad & his friend ask for the very young child | they take her to the islamic club next to that place where they sell baked eggs | a little justice: it's a world of boys & girls with noisy nokias | she's a lifted held by a world | on the fifth floor her eyes are closed now her hair thing yellow | the radio is along | we are all equally close to the good place she could be anyone | she could grow & glorious | it's an infectious world & she's of it | give us a poll give decent prediction | it's a lively prophecy infinitely slivered | the sons of noah & jacob were all told the same | of maryam & eve | be plenty | no we don't need a bench mark | a base population | to say it's A HUMAN COUNT IS CRUCIAL | revelation of that ripple that rupture | the altar of quickest way | our crusts dimming just so we bathed you in a bucket more than once child girl | that bucket was gray & black of handle & i will not forget | i come home every day & find someone who's clean | the way love takes you inside its slanted season | on the way out of me you didn't make a sound | on the balcony facing jerusalem i hear your eyelashes grow | a little justice: I HEAR YOUR EYELASHES GROW BUCKET GIRL | i still struggle to make lines longer | patience doesn't want to do its job with me right

the deepest east & dead sea & saltings on the slim | we have some times
too | i wear my eye again | i see the pupil in ink | i walk this wide way &
the heat | how this is something | joy & joy & one tyranny's smell | how
dust peels | there is a child & a chest of filial follicles | *if you move your
legs that way habibi* | how this is something | we have a roof & sufficient
serotonin & all that's human | MY NERVE ENDINGS ARE MATERIAL |
yes more like that

the more they afflicted them the more they multiplied & grew it's a census it's a disseminated population | however critically future strategies | the relatively stripped pristine | the numerically acknowledged affiliation | they census | OUR NEARLY DEMOGRAPHIC STANDING | body growth body count | affecting resolution | moving concern | suspending bordering | unsettling returning

THAT SUMMER WASN'T A PLEASANT PERSON either | summers can be drummed up to be so | teach me again to write my name in the final way | & no i don't walk like my grandfather | west bank heat like a torched tongue moves forward | eventually i will google asta olivia & find her poem on how the summer comes & fall calm in this one | on this side of the river your hands hang over a notebook & your bony pen | this afternoon & then another | i look like i didn't see that orange in your hand coming out of the snow | just like hussein always said it would

SOME STRAIGHT LINES ARE GENEROUS | some administration of population is by design | did you know that the old story of ammo amin's first wife is also the history of indigenous tuberculosis | i once saw his back spooling toward the cedars | for context i need to know more about the pre-forty-eight sanatoriums & sanatariums | i email salim | salim says see sufian & canaan | sufian works on malaria | canaan's grandson in london is still editing his grandfather's diaries | reading then was part of the cure & light | enter the children | inter the dispersed | hello enough hospital beds | one casualty post | a quarantine service at five seaports & three aerodromes including one main lazareth | then as now the last crowds are purslane & mallow | mostly mallow mighty the dead sea | slim salt | we two know | we carry our child & our

incremental emotional shifts | thank you dear i must go back | my nerve

endings are maternal | i wear my eye | i see the dissembling links | i can

weep walking | this sweet & wide occupied way | THE JOY THE FULL |

i fall headlong into | a little justice: ramallah sounds like pearls spilling

from a string

a body is a quiet choice | to say that is kinship | we walk to the top | my girl in my hand will grow tired of holding the basket of blossoms | & she says something about dinner & dying & we feel different in our throats | the school children below with their own mothers & stepmothers sail toward us | THIS HEART IS SHAPE SHIFTING every day we see hanadi | she'll soon be evicted again & she'll soon be fine again | she scoops the growing number of children into her arms | & portent lactation | in the mirror of every nearest taxi it's someone you know | on the first morning of every eid the *shabab* in crispy jeans | if you could run your hand through their composed hair | that hair wax *baladi* like THE FIGS YOU HELD | a little justice: i'll stay in this expired area | i'll bear another child fragrant dust & firstborn | this privilege inside an occupation | these old cities' distant cisterns | word of their death is exaggerated | & those children are surely eating kitkats now & following the wild dog trail in the hinterland | they play on twenty-five dunums of orange tree & olive tree | nabila waits for her husband to arrive late for supper | ribbons hang & fruit wrapping paper in some haberdashery | HOME IS EQUAL PARTS ARCHITECTURAL & GUTTURAL | our ripple ripens hereditary it's a rain & you were born before it | you were born in your body | just like that | no one refutes these areas were made to carry letters & the letters lapsed | in a world of fewer babies you were born | dear RIOT COSMOLOGY | i never thought i'd be a national vessel | febrile & inlaid | undulating so | we worked hard to be fruitful & plenty

BIRTH IS A SOCIAL PROCESS | have i seen how it's hot & all the ways i resist it | have i remembered fatma in a kitchen & the way she was somebody near | i never thought i'd one day forget her smell or quite recover | today a new spreading in my interior body | today is reorienting | belly bloom | yes israel has a fertility treatment rate that is thirteen times the united states level per capita | you relish these native olives bucket girl & it's a little justice | palestinians have a way with children too | & YOU ARE SOMETHING STUNNING

THEY SAID IT WAS MORNING | i translate a poem in vatic light from jericho | stay human says the wall | i loop like the smoke rolling still in your mouth | the street becomes a street that fills up with spring & sheep curbs & carob trees | i stretch my right knee | at home a new child waits along with blue eyes & hair | where she is born is a fine thing | *scabiosa palestina* | i need to put a load in the washer | i don't always look up when you walk by | collected grafted | warm root | i feel possibly covered like a book drawn in that coffee shop for men | & then i feel right in every corner like a table

NOTES

20 The language has been adapted from the Palestinian Central Bureau of Statistics annual demographic report: PCBS: The Palestinians at the End of 2014.

28 The language has been adapted from the 2016 annual demographic report by Israel's Central Bureau of Statistics.

32 "now hannah she spoke in her heart…" from 1 Samuel 1:1-1:20 on Hannah's barrenness and prayer to arouse divine compassion for her plight. Various midrashim address how Hannah attempts to persuade God to enable her to bear children. The language here borrows from BT Berakhot 31b.

36 "& peace will be on you…" echoes Surat Maryam 19:33

39 "although seabird populations can withstand the failure to produce young..." from G.L. Hunt Jr, in Encyclopedia of Ocean Sciences, 2nd ed., 2001.

42 During Israel's three-week assault on Gaza in December 2008-January 2009, known as Operation Cast Lead, more than 1400 Palestinians lost their lives. The vast majority, 1200, were civilians. The Samouni family lost 23 members of its extended family in two days.

42 & 52 "there is something out there i'm trying to catch" from Kristine Kemp, tSSoP Papers, Copenhagen 2011, [Der er noget derude jeg prøver at gribe... Netop nu spreder Daniel ko-pis på sine græsmarker. Han pløjer dem med det samme, så den ubehagelige stank af råddent æg hurtigt fordufter.]

45 "... for seabirds the aggregation of large portions of the adult population in colonies …" G.L. Hunt Jr., ibid.

47 "and the pains of childbirth drove her to the trunk of a palm tree…" From Surat Maryam 19:23-26.

48 "our divine guardian rock & redeemer of | …" adapts language from the first line of "Prayer for Peace in the State of Israel" 1948. A founding text of Israeli and Hebrew liturgy, academics have disagreed for decades whether to attribute the text to Nobel Prize winning writer S.Y Agnon or first chief Ashkenazi Rabbi Isaac Halevi Herzog.

50 "o my lord i have vowed to you what is in my womb…" From Surat 'Imran 3:35.

51 "we exist... [& die].. to introduce even a minimal change in the strength of the state" borrows its language from Michel Foucault, Technologies of the Self, 1988:151.

54 The phrase "twenty impossibles" is from Tawfiq Zayyad's 1965 poem "hunā bāqūna" [here we shall remain]; and the line "we are all equally close to the good places" echoes the title of Adania Shibli's 2004 novella "kullu-nā baʿīd bi-dhāt al-miqdār ʿan al-hubb" [we are all equally far from love].

58 "the more they afflicted them, the more they multiplied" from Exodus 1:12.

60 The line "that orange in your hand coming out of the snow" paraphrases a line from Hussein al-Barghouthi's 2002 poem "ḥajar al-ward" [the rosetta stone].

ACKNOWLEDGMENTS

Poems from this collection appear in *Berkeley Poetry Review*, *jubilat*, and the *Laurel Review*. Thank you to the editors and readers of these publications. I am grateful to Gillian Hamel, Kayla Ellenbecker, Ken Keegan, and everyone at Omnidawn for such careful midwifery of this book, and to judge Dawn Lundy Martin for hearing its call. Special gratitude to editors and poets Rusty Morrison and Caryl Pagel for first words of seeing that meant so much to me.

Thank you from my heart to Kifah Fanni, Palestinian poet and old friend. It took a while. For reading and rooting for early and late versions of this collection, thank you so much Anna Ghosh, Nora El Samahy, Laura Walker, Bill Parry, Lotte Buch Segal, Irene Siegel, Norma Cole, Chana Kronfeld, and Debra Bronstein.

Tak Kristine Kemp for that old bridge, although I never saw Vallarum and you never saw Ramallah. For your close companionship in Palestine, and your footsteps in and around these poems: Sharry Lapp, Maissoun Sharkawi, Rana Barakat, Abeer Musleh, Susan Rockwell, Shirabe Yamada, Awatef Sheikh, Jeanine Shama, Abeer Habash, and Jessika Devlieghere. Hanadi Kobari, for loving our riots as your own. For your friendship, helping me land softly: Jumana Muwafi, Emily Katz, Houda Soubra, and Mona Masri.

To my parents Irja and Fayez Khankan and sister Sherin Khankan for your unwavering support and love.

To Basil Ayish, abu Yara and Luma, who makes buttertime possible anywhere. Just like that. JED. To Yara and Luma, this book is also a birth map. This is where you were born and so loved.

Nathalie Khankan was born in Copenhagen, Denmark. Her poems appear in the *Berkeley Poetry Review*, *jubilat*, and *Crab Creek Review*. She was the founding director of The Danish House in Palestine and now teaches Arabic language and literature in the Department of Near Eastern Studies at the University of California, Berkeley. Straddling Danish, Finnish, Syrian and Palestinian homes and heirlooms, Nathalie currently lives in San Francisco.

quiet orient riot
Nathalie Khankan

Cover art by: Bashir Makhoul, *One drop of my tears*, 2000
Photograph, 200cm x 200cm

Cover and interior set in Poiret One, Kabel LT Std, and Electra LT Std

Cover and interior design by Gillian Olivia Blythe Hamel

Printed in the United States
by Bookmobile, Minneapolis, Minnesota
On Rolland Enviro Book 70# 392 ppi Natural 100% PCW
Acid Free Archival Quality Recycled Paper

Publication of this book was made possible in part by gifts from
Katherine & John Gravendyk in honor of Hillary Gravendyk,
Francesca Bell, Mary Mackey, and The New Place Fund

Omnidawn Publishing
Oakland, California
Staff and Volunteers, Fall 2020

Rusty Morrison & Ken Keegan, senior editors & co-publishers
Kayla Ellenbecker, production editor & poetry editor
Gillian Olivia Blythe Hamel, senior editor & book designer
Trisha Peck, senior editor & book designer
Rob Hendricks, *Omniverse* editor, marketing editor & post-pub editor
Cassandra Smith, poetry editor & book designer
Sharon Zetter, poetry editor & book designer
Liza Flum, poetry editor
Matthew Bowie, poetry editor
Jason Bayani, poetry editor
Juliana Paslay, fiction editor
Gail Aronson, fiction editor
Izabella Santana, fiction editor & marketing assistant
Laura Joakimson, marketing assistant specializing in Instagram & Facebook
Ashley Pattison-Scott, executive assistant & *Omniverse* writer
Ariana Nevarez, marketing assistant & *Omniveres* writer
SD Sumner, copyeditor